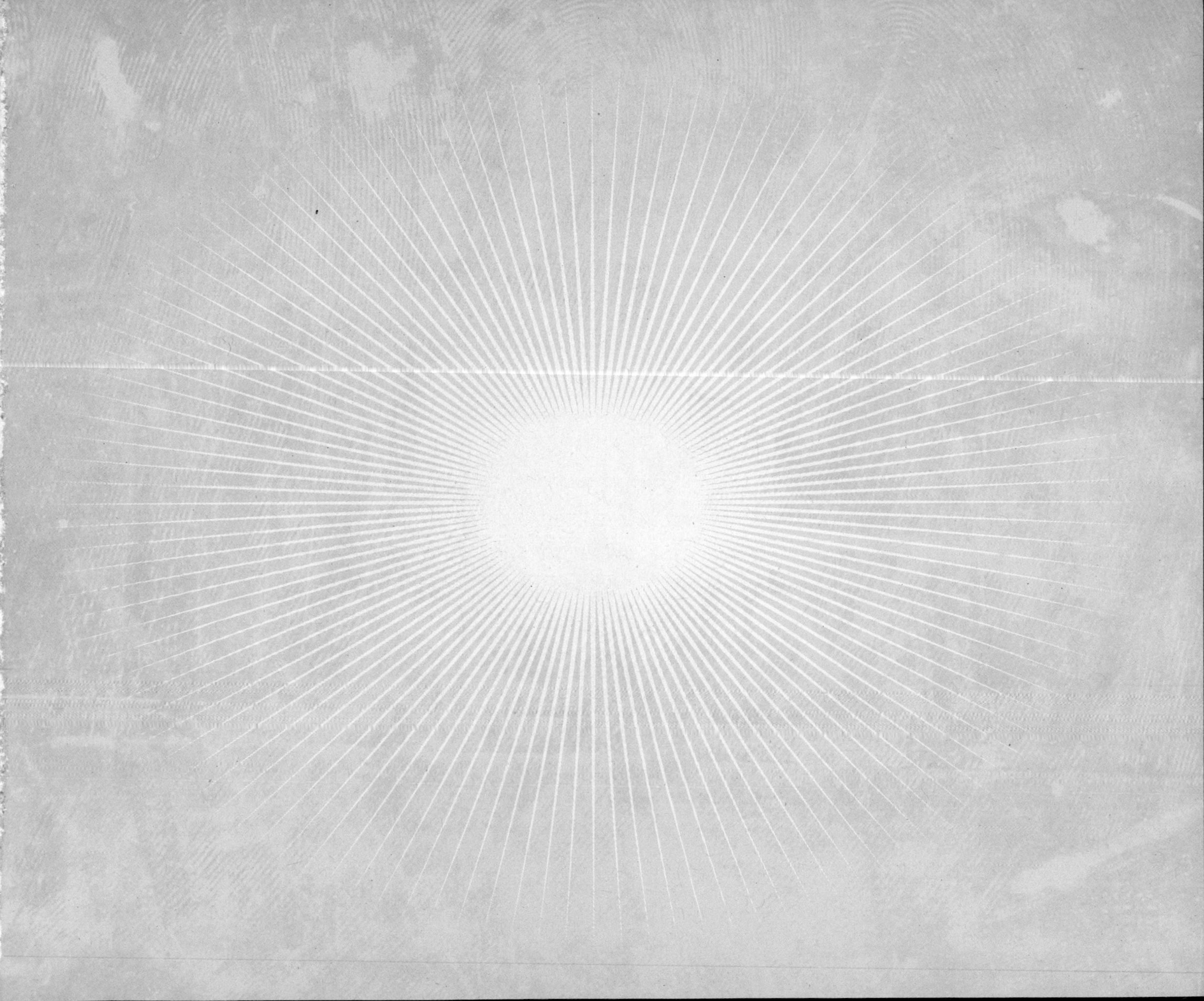

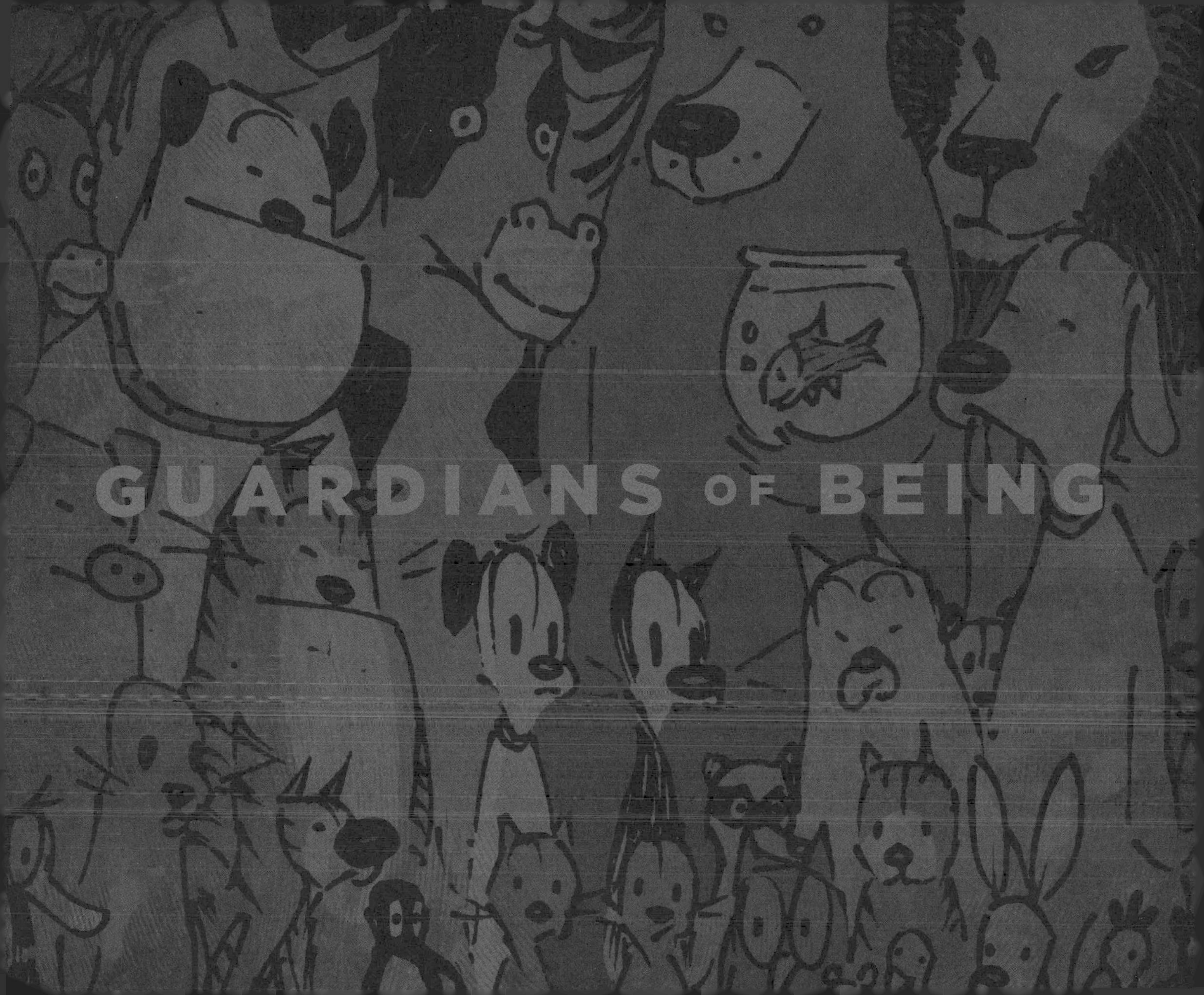
GUARDIANS OF BEING

GUARDIANS OF BEING

WORDS BY **ECKHART TOLLE** ART BY **PATRICK McDONNELL**

New World Library
Novato, California

New World Library
14 Pamaron Way
Novato, California 94949

Book design by Jeff Schulz / Command-Z Design

Library of Congress Cataloging-in-Publication Data

Tolle, Eckhart
Guardians of being / words by Eckhart Tolle ; art by Patrick McDonnell.
p. cm.
ISBN 978-1-57731-671-8 (hardcover : alk. paper)
1. Spiritual life. 2. Comic books, strips, etc. I. McDonnell, Patrick, 1956– II. Title.
BL624.T633 2009
204'.4—dc22 2009020388

First printing, August 2009
ISBN 978-1-57731-671-8
Printed in Canada on 100% postconsumer-waste recycled paper

New World Library is a proud member of the Green Press Initiative.

Mixed Sources
Product group from well-managed forests, controlled sources and recycled wood or fiber
www.fsc.org Cert no. SW-COC-000952
© 1996 Forest Stewardship Council
FSC

98%

10 9 8 7 6 5 4 3 2 1

True happiness is found in simple, seemingly unremarkable things.

But to be aware of little, quiet things,
you need to be quiet inside.

A high degree of alertness is required.

Be still. Look. Listen.

Be present.

Bring awareness to the many subtle sounds of nature —

the rustling of leaves in the wind,

raindrops falling,

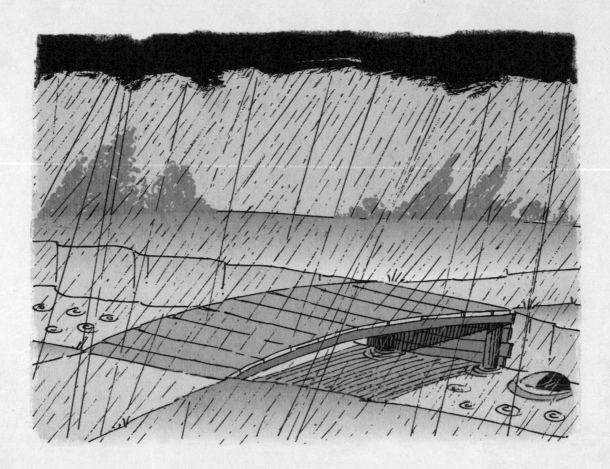

the humming of an insect,

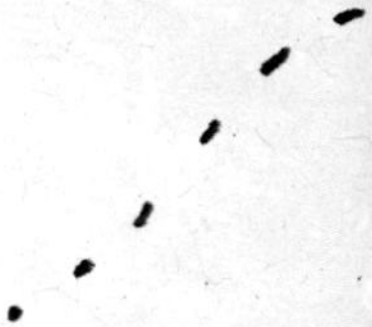

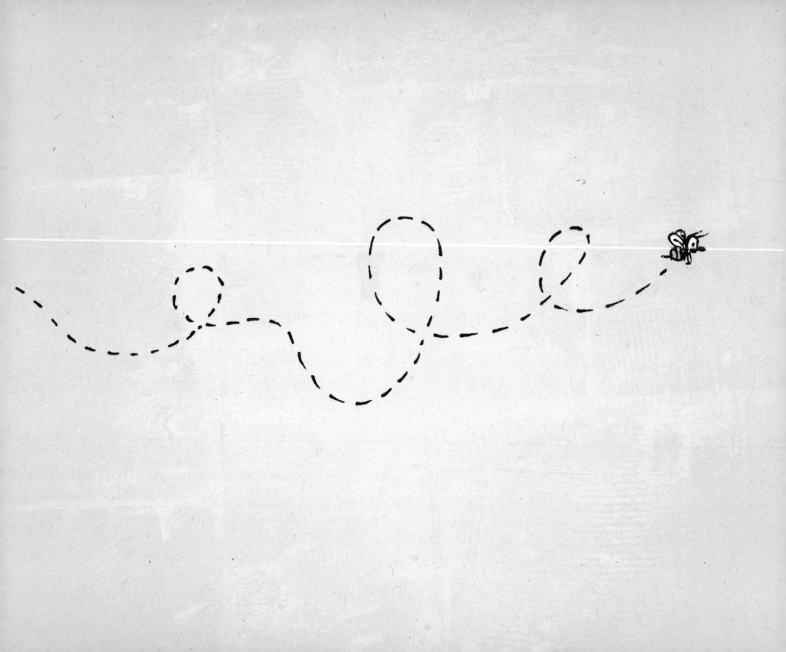

the first birdsong at dawn.

Give yourself completely

to the act of listening.

Beyond the sounds

there is something greater:

a sacredness that cannot be

understood through thought.

Look at a tree, a flower, a plant.

Let your awareness rest upon it.

How still it is, how deeply rooted in Being.

Allow nature to teach you stillness.

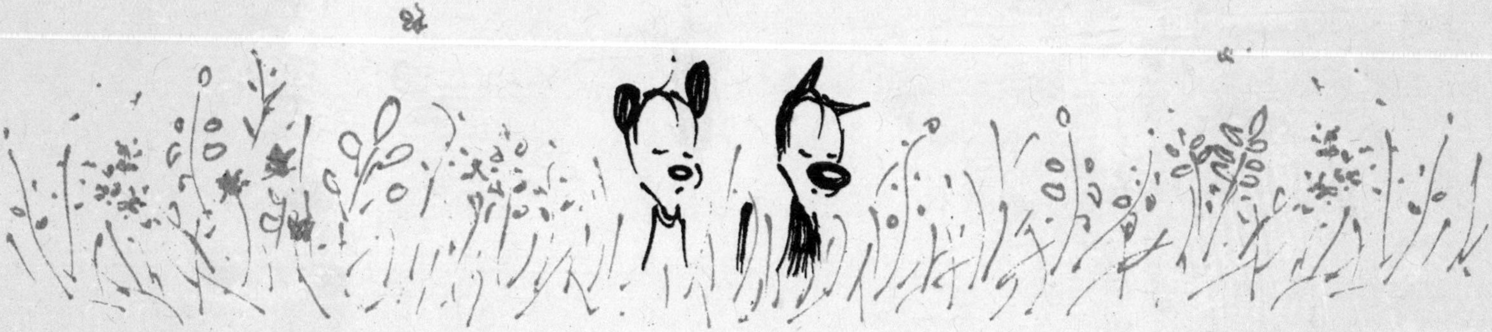

Everything natural — every flower, tree,
and animal — has important
lessons to teach us if we would only
stop, look, and listen.

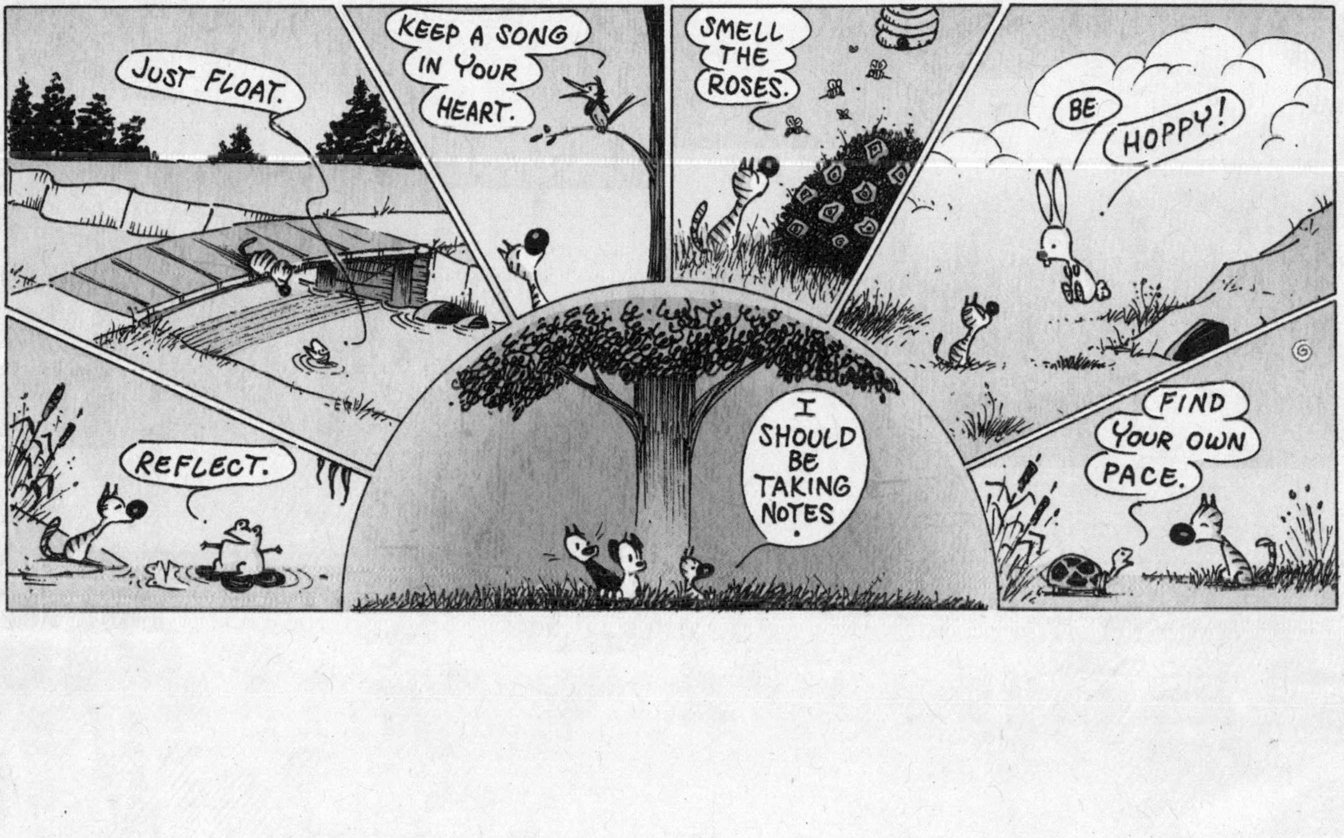
JUST FLOAT.
KEEP A SONG IN YOUR HEART.
SMELL THE ROSES.
BE HOPPY!
REFLECT.
I SHOULD BE TAKING NOTES.
FIND YOUR OWN PACE.

Just watching an animal closely can take you out of
your mind and bring you into the present moment,
which is where the animal lives all the time —

surrendered to life.

It's so wonderful to watch an animal,
because an animal has no opinion about itself.

It is.

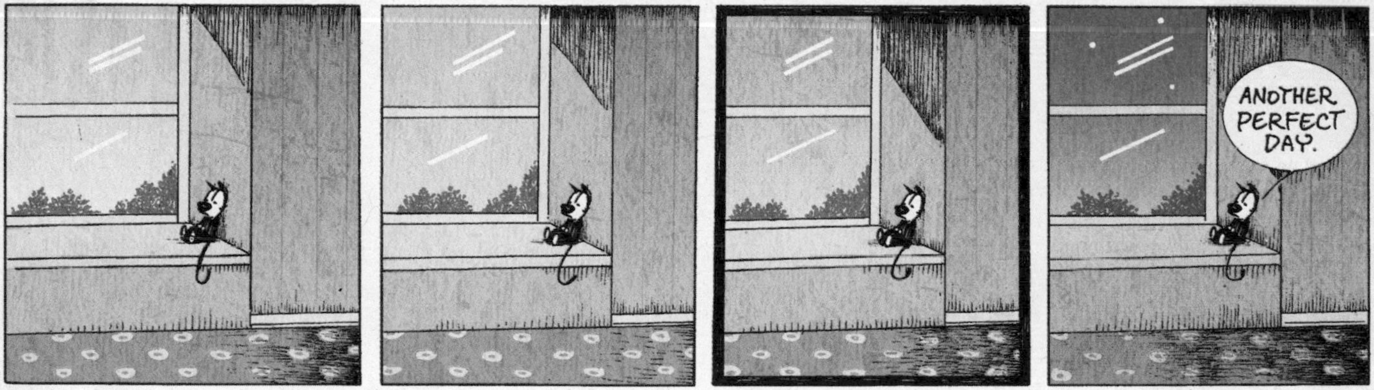
ANOTHER PERFECT DAY.

That's why the dog is so joyful

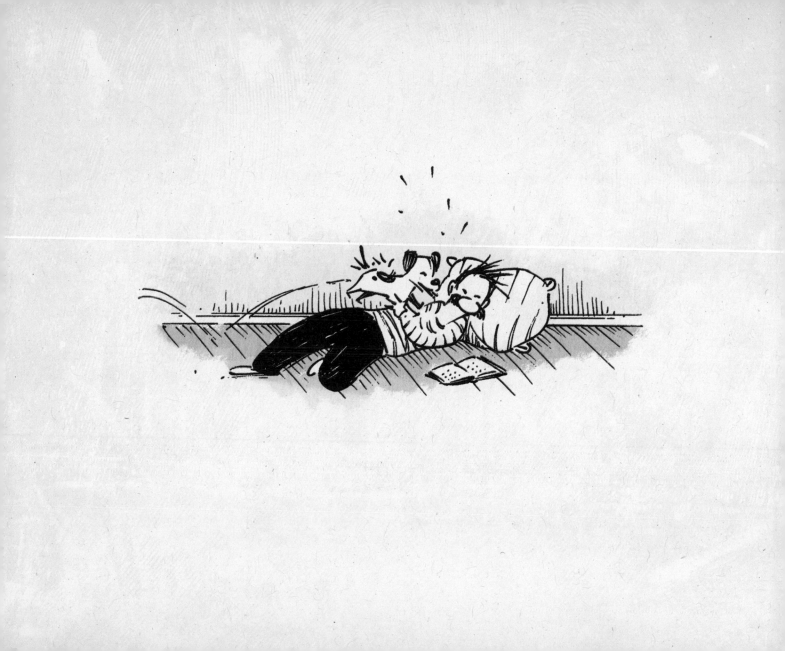

and why the cat purrs.

PURRRR

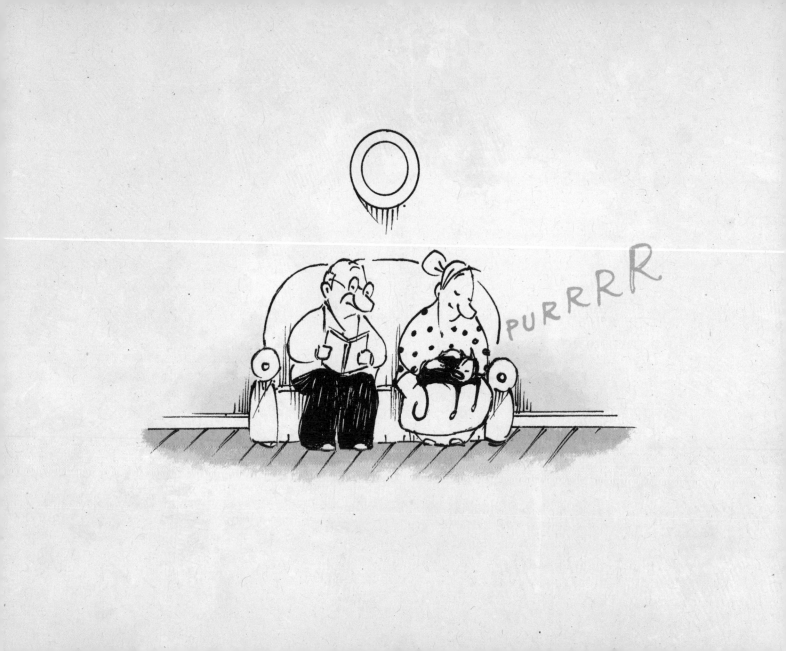

When you pet a dog or listen to a cat purring,
thinking may subside for a moment and

a space of stillness

arises within you, a doorway into Being.

The vital function that pets fulfill in this world hasn't been fully recognized. They keep millions of people sane.

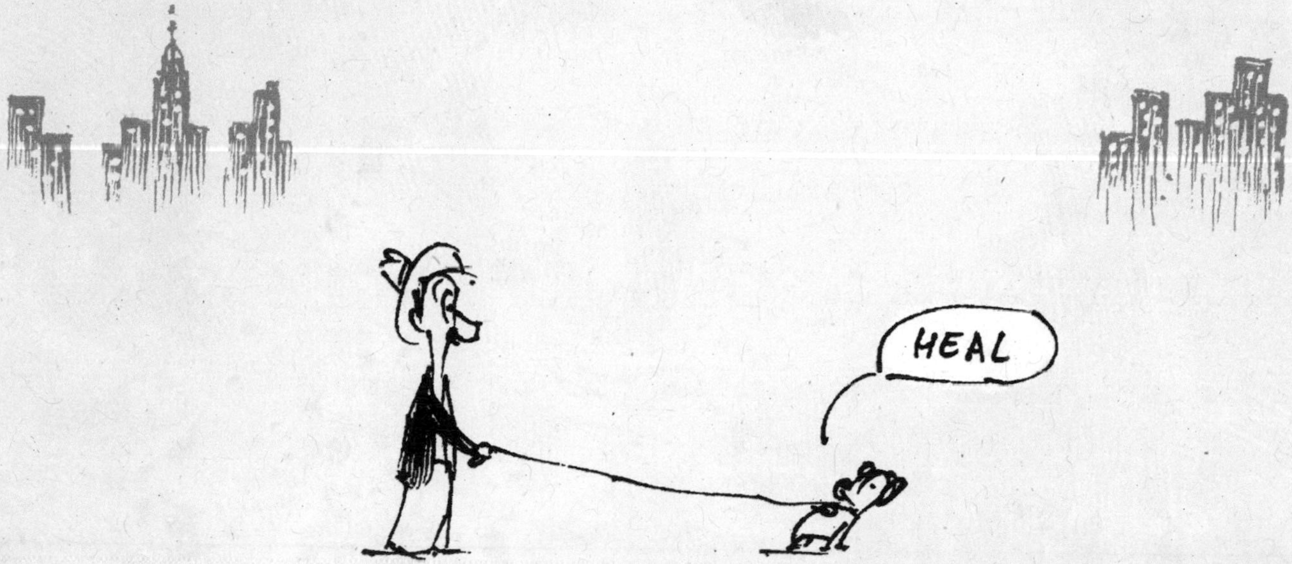
HEAL

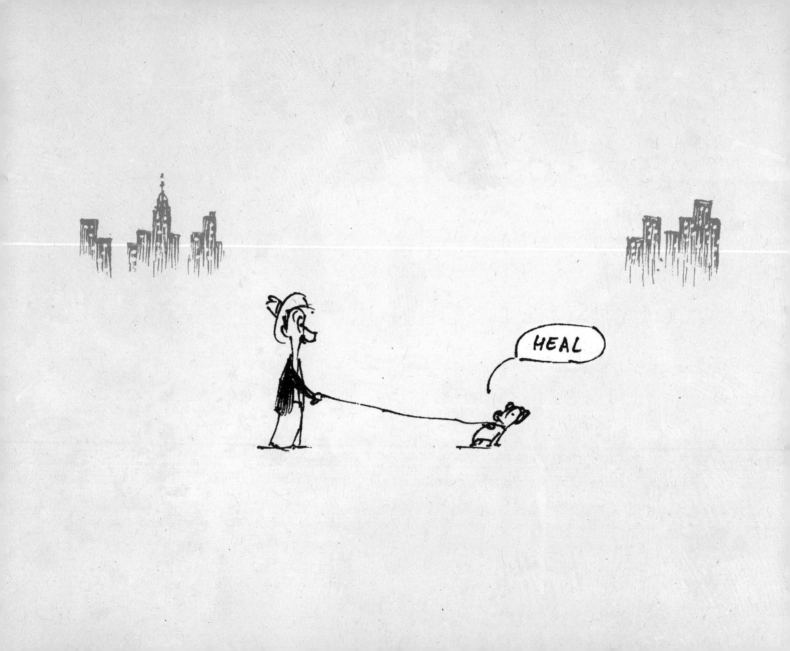

They have become Guardians of Being.

Most of us live in a world of

mental abstraction, conceptualization,

and image making — a world of thought.

We are immersed in a continuous stream

of mental noise. It seems that we can't

stop thinking.

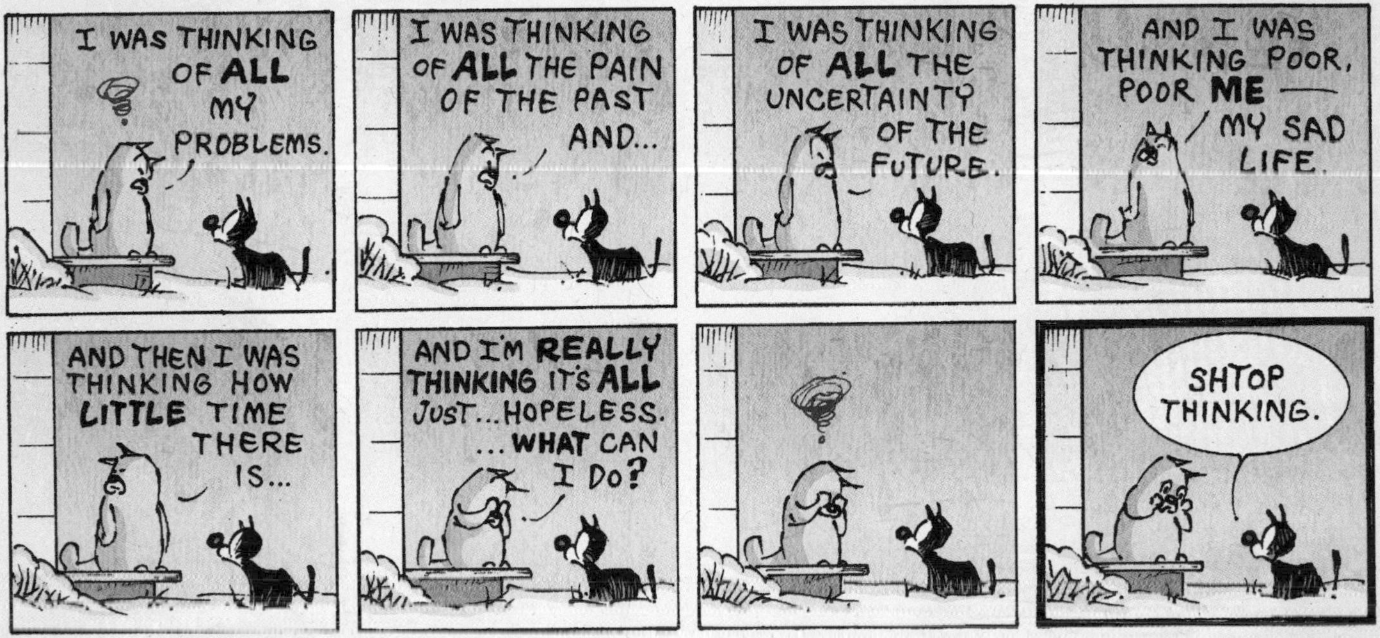
I WAS THINKING OF ALL MY PROBLEMS.
I WAS THINKING OF ALL THE PAIN OF THE PAST AND...
I WAS THINKING OF ALL THE UNCERTAINTY OF THE FUTURE.
AND I WAS THINKING POOR, POOR ME — MY SAD LIFE.
AND THEN I WAS THINKING HOW LITTLE TIME THERE IS...
AND I'M REALLY THINKING IT'S ALL JUST...HOPELESS. ...WHAT CAN I DO?
SHTOP THINKING.

Just as the dog

loves to chew bones,

the human mind

loves its problems.

SQUEEK SQUEEK
SQUEEK SQUEEK
SQUEEK SQUEEK
SQUEEK SQUEEK SQUEEK
SQUEEK SQUEEK SQUEEK
SQUEEK SQUEEK
SQUEEK SQUEEK
SQUEEK SQUEEK
"FUN" FOR THE WHOLE FAMILY.

We get lost in doing, thinking, remembering, anticipating —

lost in a maze of complexity and a world of problems.

Nature can show us the way home,

the way out of the prison of our own minds.

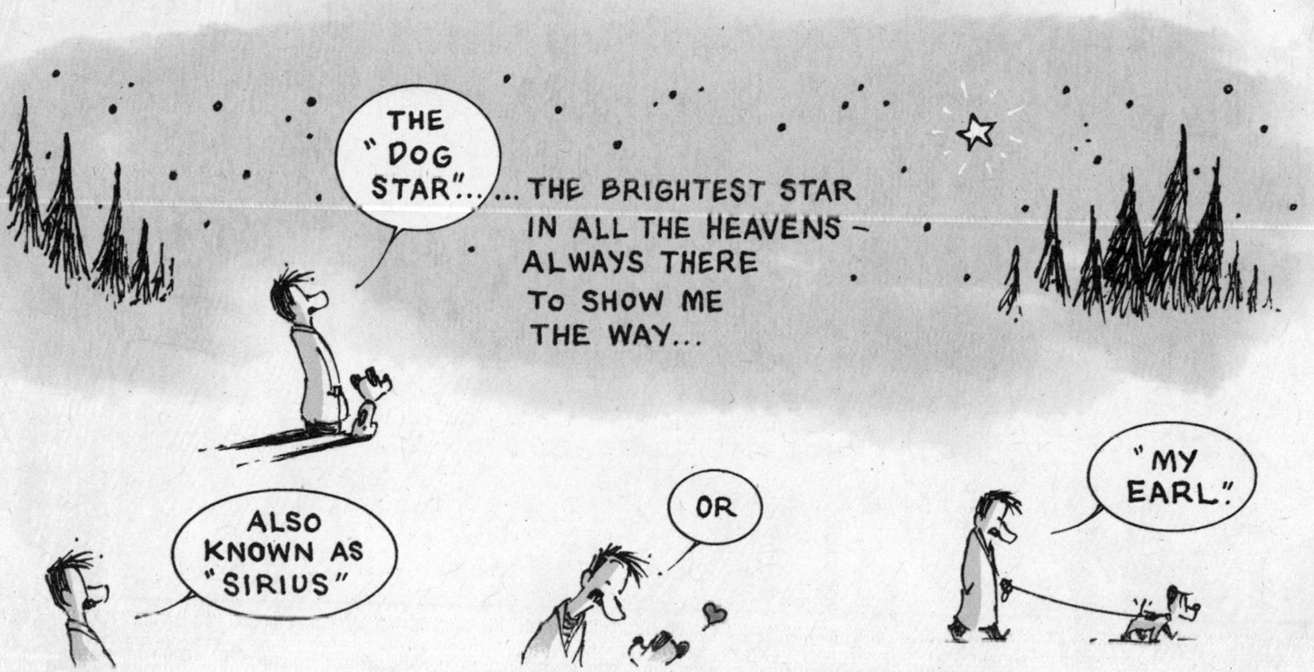
THE "DOG STAR"...
... THE BRIGHTEST STAR IN ALL THE HEAVENS – ALWAYS THERE TO SHOW ME THE WAY...
ALSO KNOWN AS "SIRIUS"
OR
"MY EARL."

Close your eyes and say to yourself:

"I wonder what my next thought is going to be."

Then become as alert as a cat watching a mouse hole.

You may find that, as long as you are absolutely alert,

the next thought does not arise. . . .

WAITING FOR THE MOUSE.

WAITING, FOR THE MOUSE.

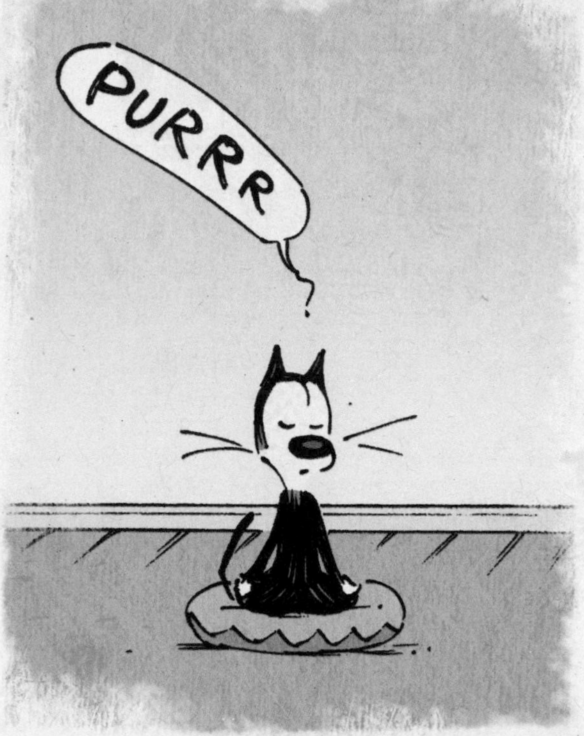
PURRR

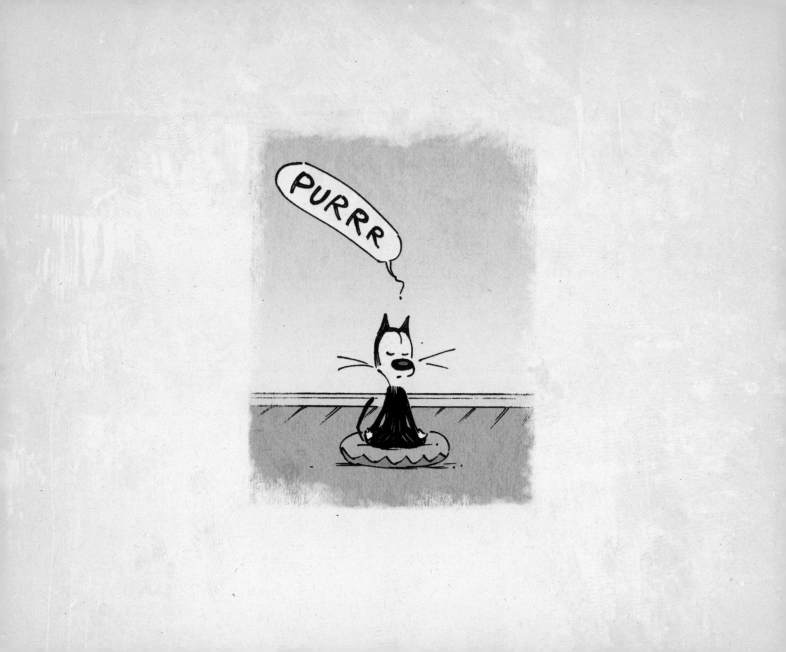

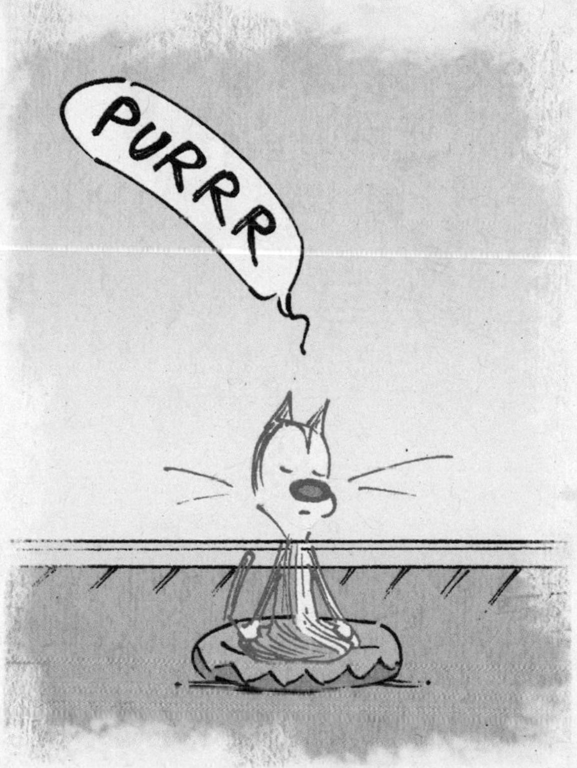
PURRR

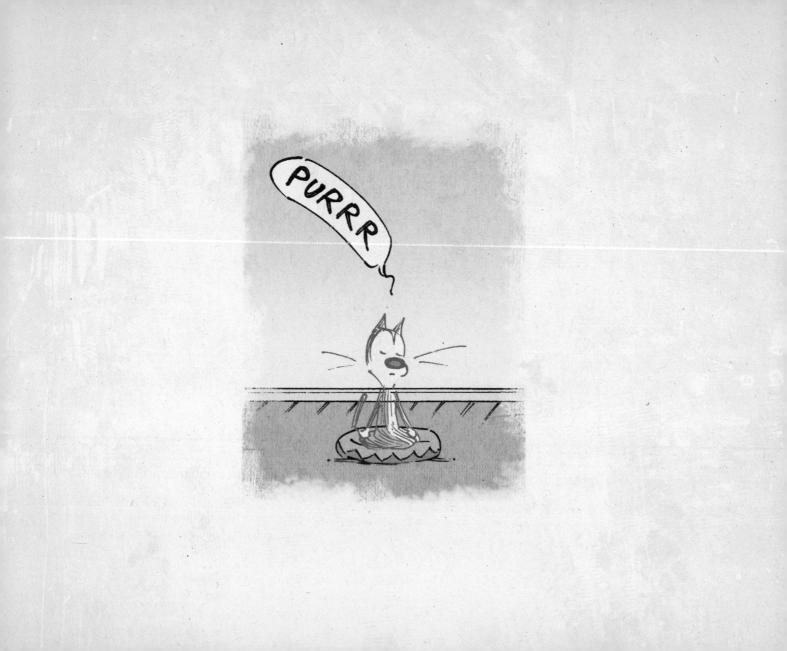

I have lived

with many

Zen masters,

all of them cats.

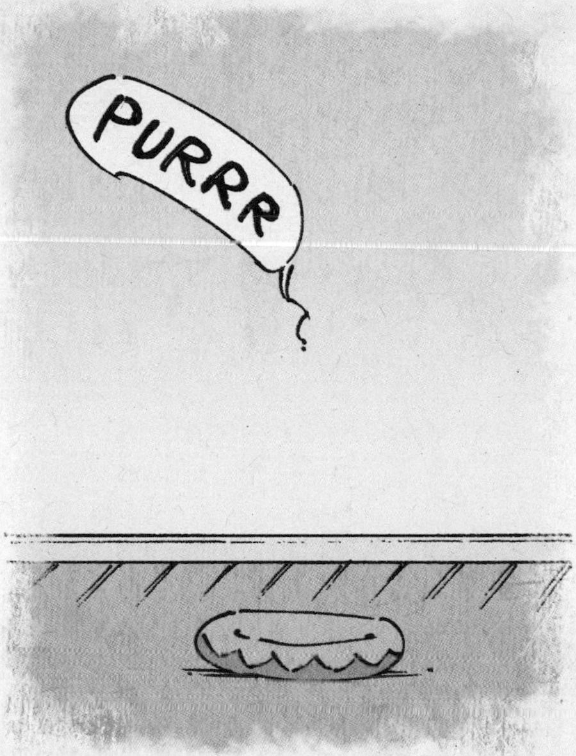
PURRR

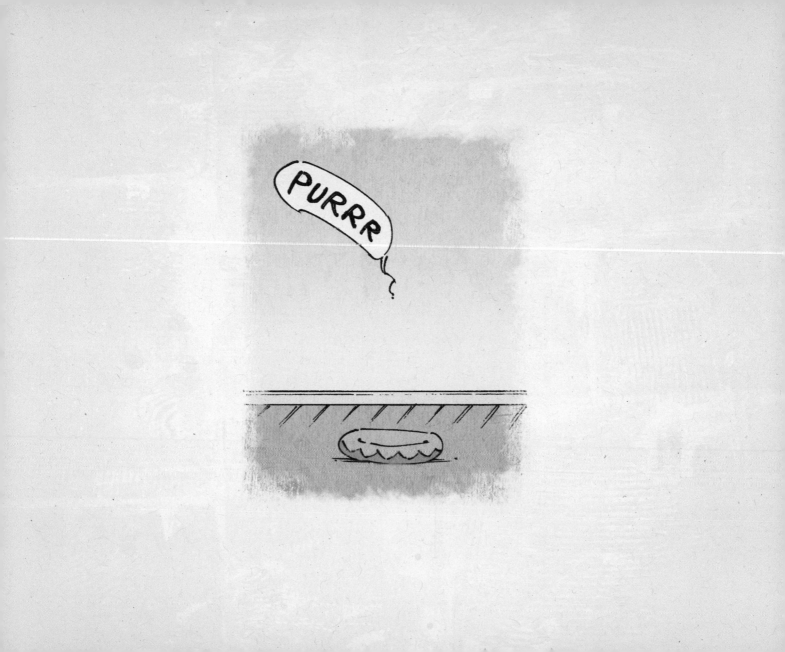

Millions of people who otherwise would be completely lost in their minds and in endless past and future concerns are taken back by their dog or cat into the present moment, again and again, and reminded of the joy of Being.

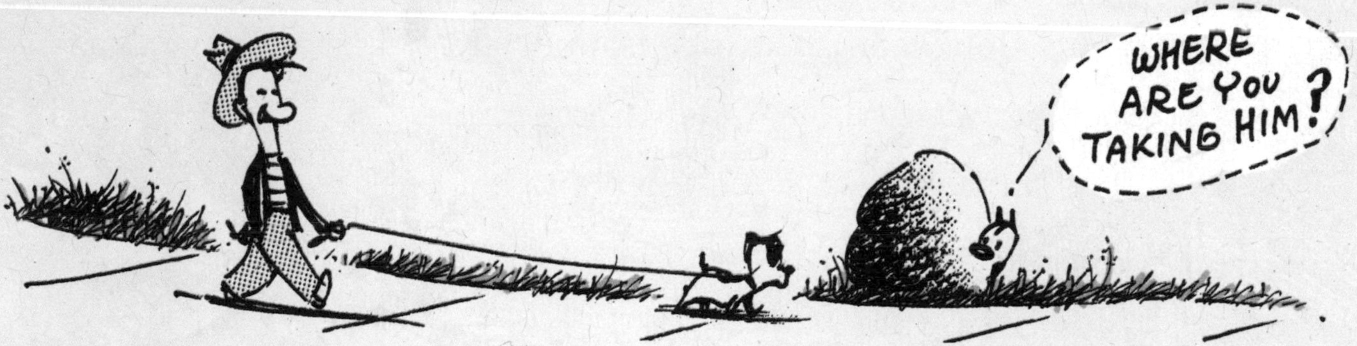
WHERE ARE YOU TAKING HIM?

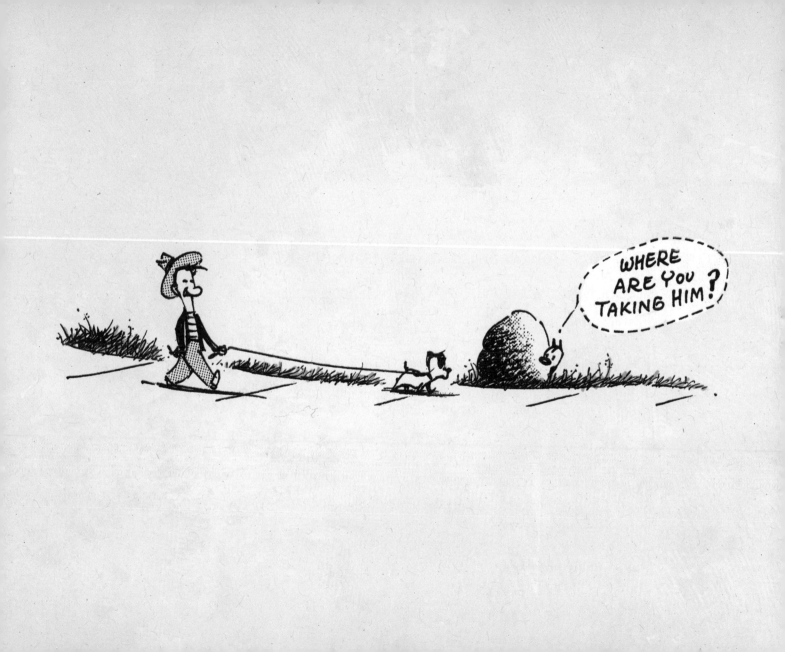

We have forgotten what rocks, plants, and
animals still know. We have forgotten how to be —
to be still, to be ourselves, to be where life is:

Here and Now.

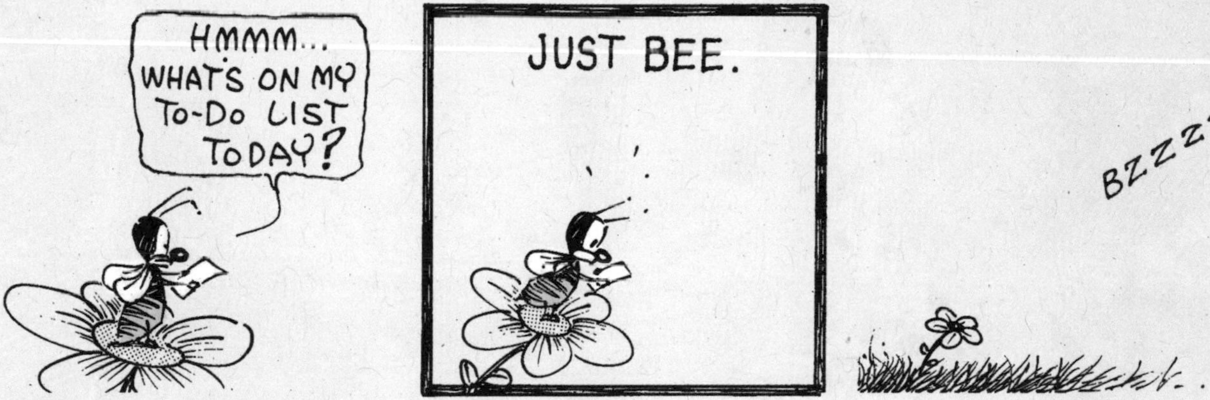
HMMM... WHAT'S ON MY TO-DO LIST TODAY?
JUST BEE.
BZZZZ.

The dog is in the Now

so it can teach you or remind you.

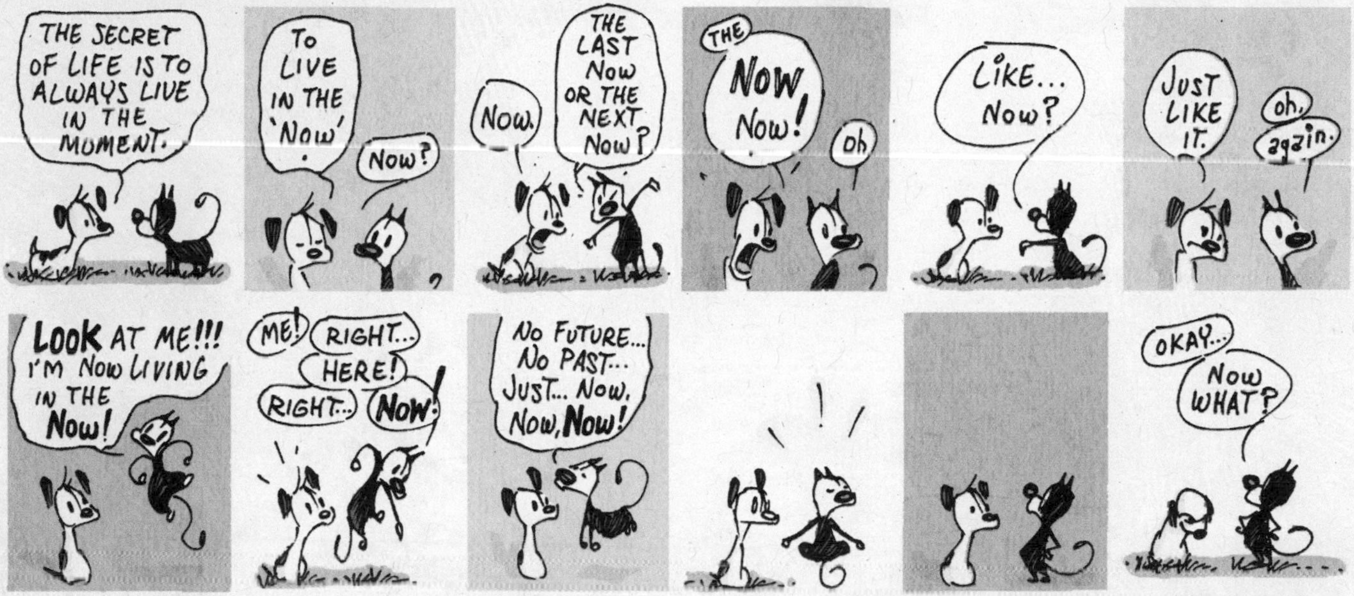
THE SECRET OF LIFE IS TO ALWAYS LIVE IN THE MOMENT.
TO LIVE IN THE 'NOW'.
NOW?
NOW.
THE LAST NOW OR THE NEXT NOW?
THE
NOW, NOW!
oh
LIKE... NOW?
JUST LIKE IT.
oh, again.
LOOK AT ME!!! I'M NOW LIVING IN THE NOW!
ME!
RIGHT...
HERE!
RIGHT...
NOW!
NO FUTURE... NO PAST... JUST... NOW. NOW, NOW!
OKAY...
NOW WHAT?

Be alert as you watch a dog at play or at rest.

Let the animal teach you to feel at home in the Now, to

celebrate life by being

completely present.

The dog is still in the natural state. And you can easily see that, because you have problems and your dog doesn't. And while your happy moments may be rare, your dog celebrates life continuously.

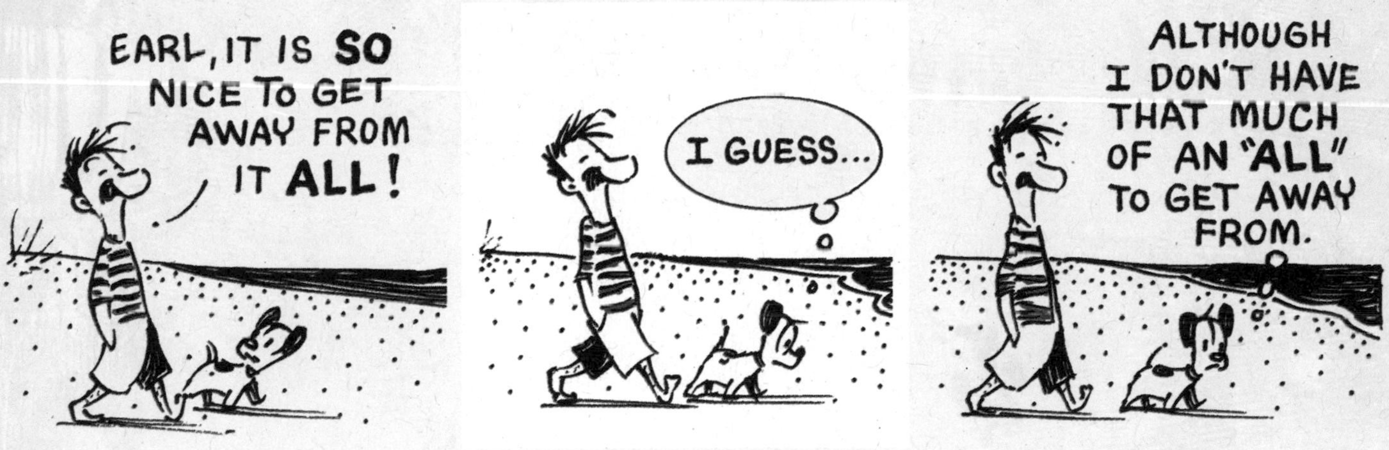
EARL, IT IS SO NICE TO GET AWAY FROM IT ALL!
I GUESS...
ALTHOUGH I DON'T HAVE THAT MUCH OF AN "ALL" TO GET AWAY FROM.

You just watch the tail...

with some dogs you just look at them —

just a little look is enough — and their tail goes...

"Life is good! Life is good!"

And they are not telling themselves a story of *why* life is good.

It's a direct realization.

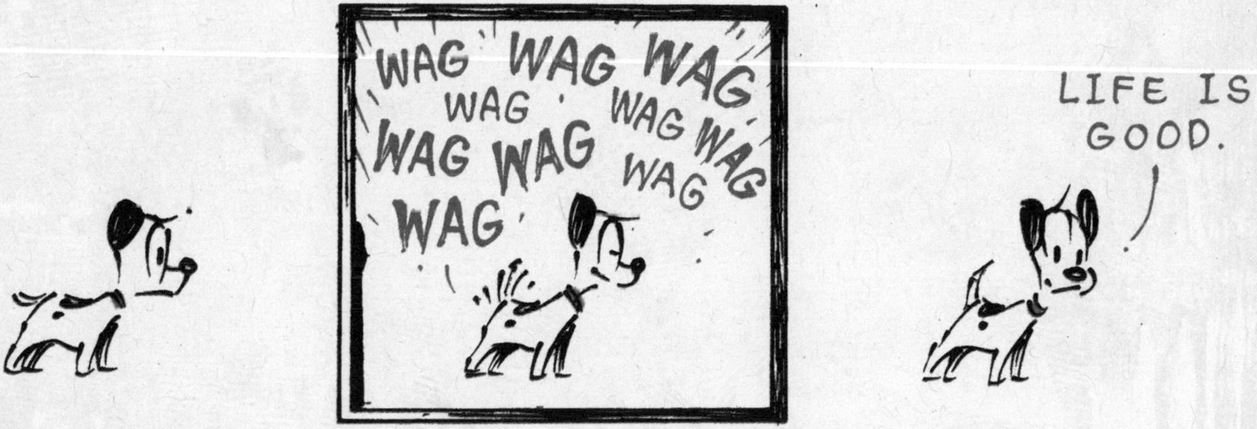

WAG WAG WAG
WAG WAG WAG
WAG WAG WAG WAG
WAG
LIFE IS GOOD.

The human says, "I love myself," or, "I hate myself."

The dog says, "Woof, woof," which, translated, means

I am myself.

I call that integrity — being one with yourself.

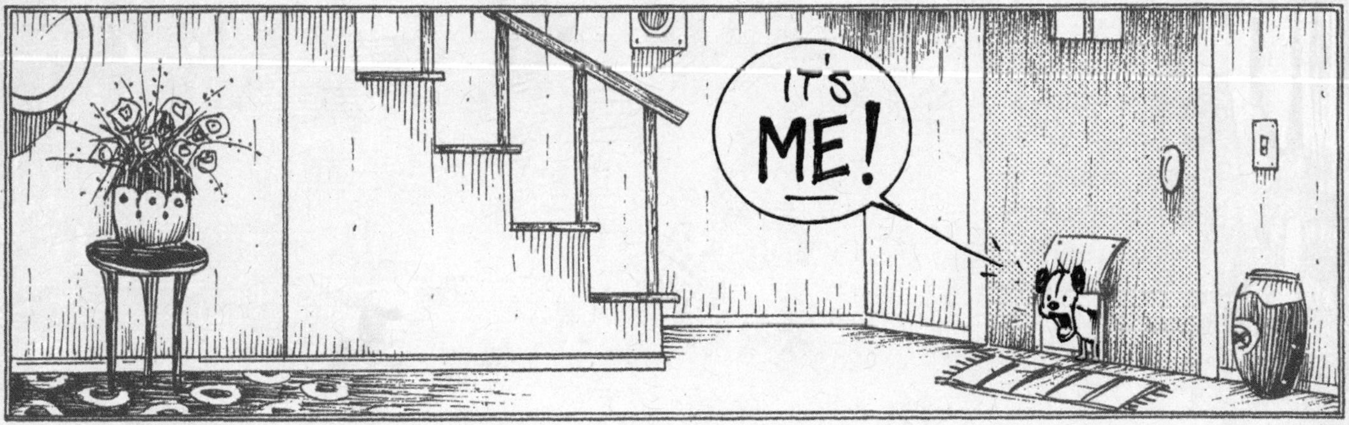
IT'S ME!

The dog has no self-image, good or bad,

so he has no need to play roles,

nor does he love himself or hate himself.

He has no self!

How to live free of the burden of self —

what a great spiritual teaching.

EAT.
WALK.
PLAY.
NAP.
I'M A SIMPLE DOG.

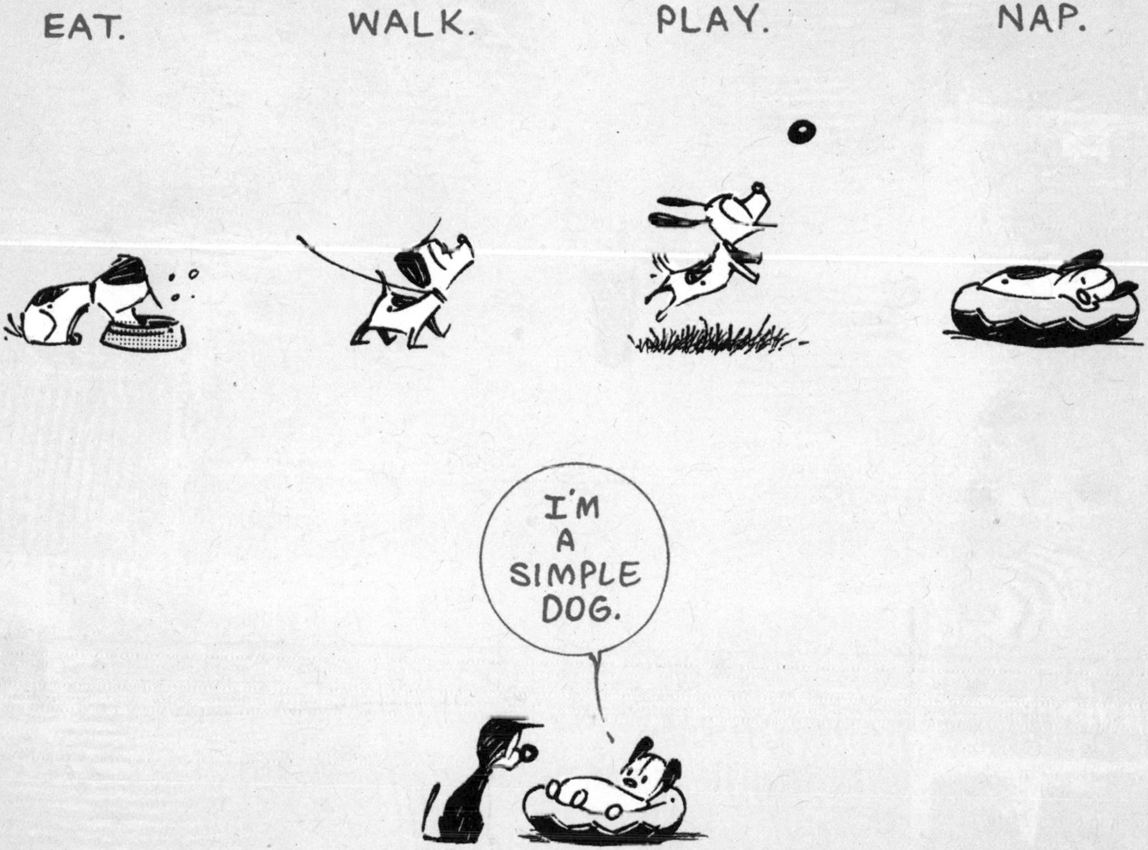

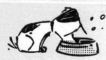

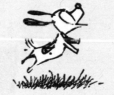

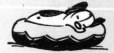

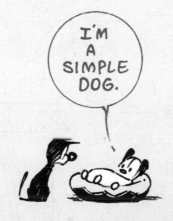

"The key to transformation is to
make friends with this moment.
What form it takes doesn't matter.
Say yes to it. Allow it. Be with it."

Oh, that was the dog's teaching.
I'm just translating it into words.

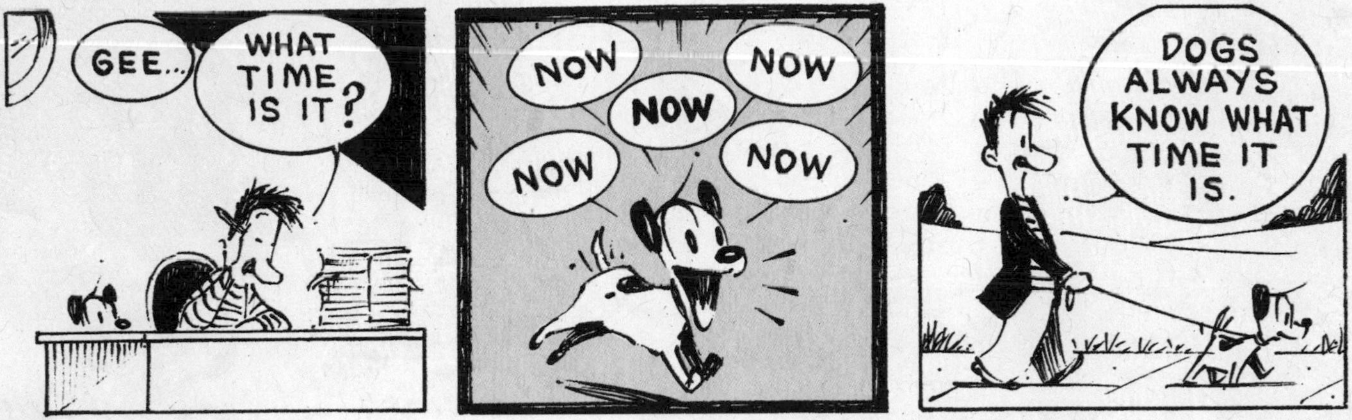
GEE...
WHAT TIME IS IT?
NOW
NOW
NOW
NOW
NOW
DOGS ALWAYS KNOW WHAT TIME IT IS.

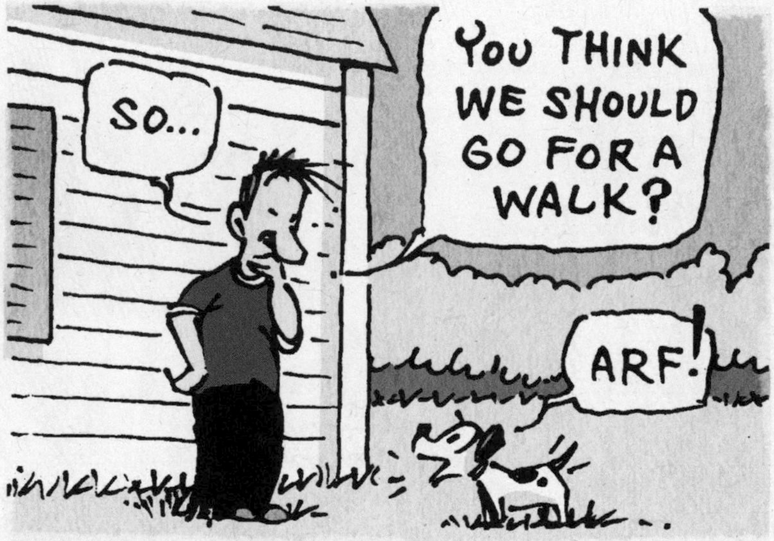
SO...
YOU THINK WE SHOULD GO FOR A WALK?
ARF!

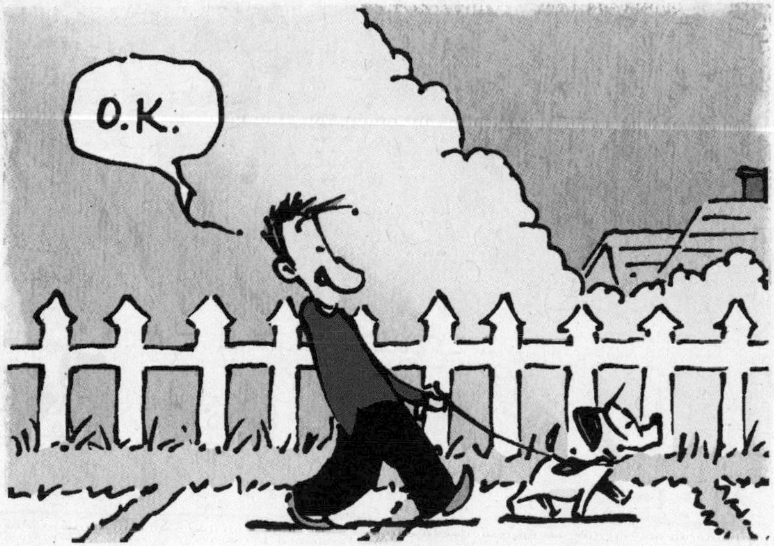
O.K.

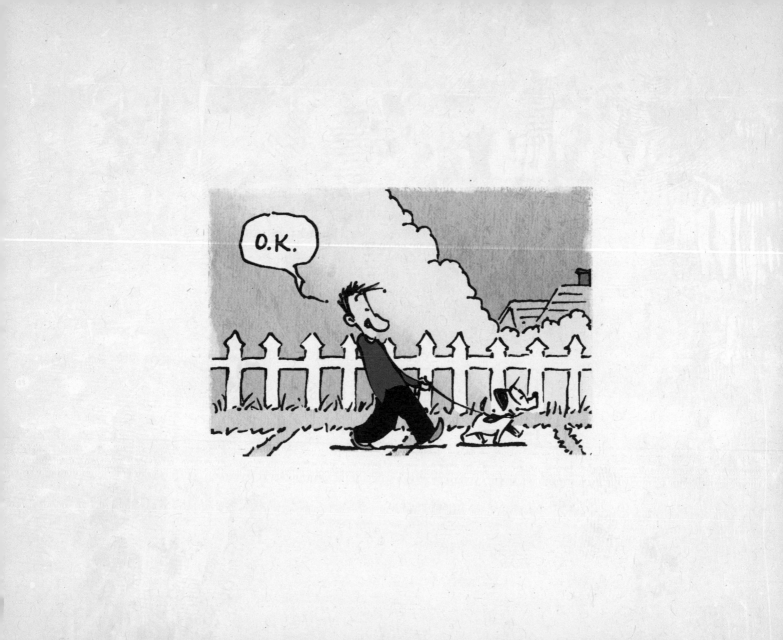

Allow your dog to

take you for a walk every day.

It's good for the body and

it's good for the soul.

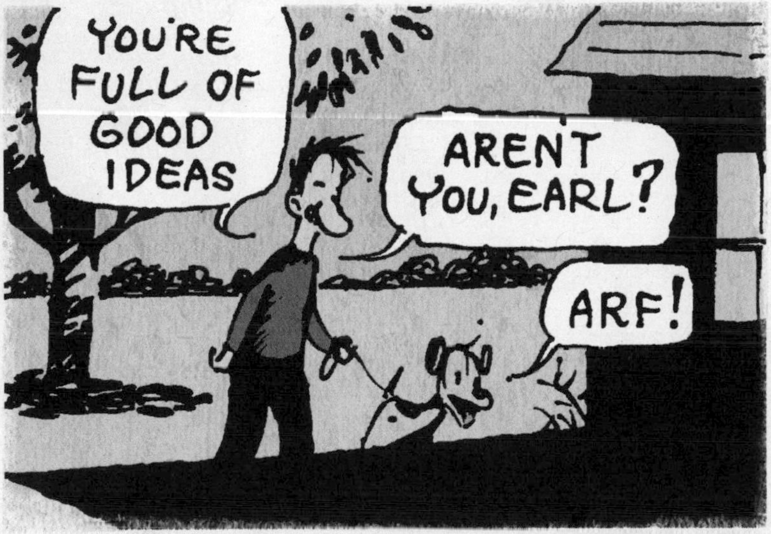
YOU'RE FULL OF GOOD IDEAS
ARENT YOU, EARL?
ARF!

Dogs emanate a goodness that people respond to.

One of the joys of walking your dog is that often people

come up to you and immediately their hearts open.

They are not interested in you, of course.

They want to pat your dog.

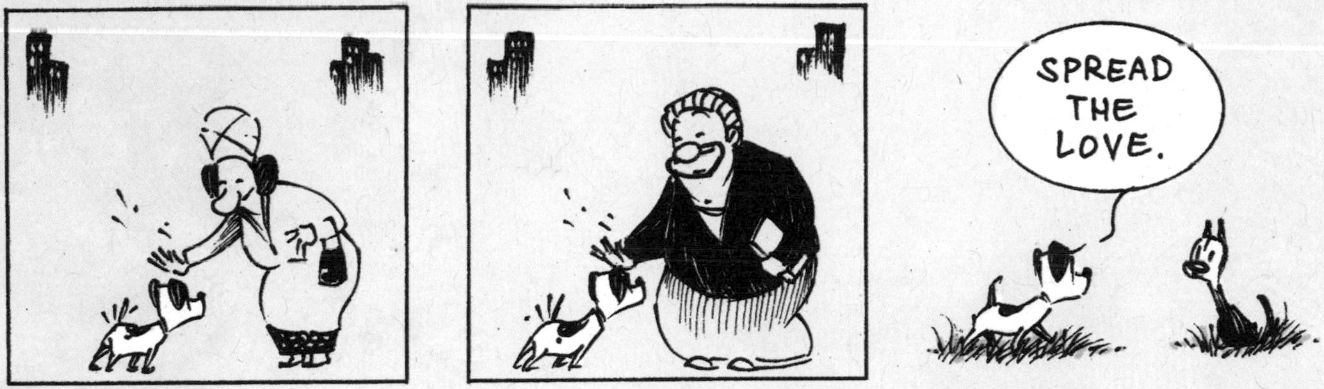
SPREAD THE LOVE.

Dogs offer the precious opportunity,

even to people who are trapped in their egos,

of loving and being loved unconditionally.

DINNER.
GOOD BOY.

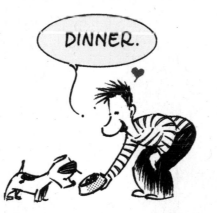

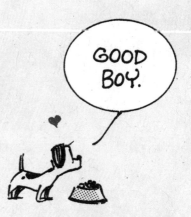

They have been with humans for thousands of years, and now
there is a link between dogs and humans,
much closer than it has ever been.

I'M **NEVER** 'OFF LEASH'
WITH MY OZZIE...
OUR HEARTS ARE CONNECTED.

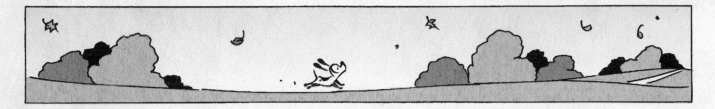

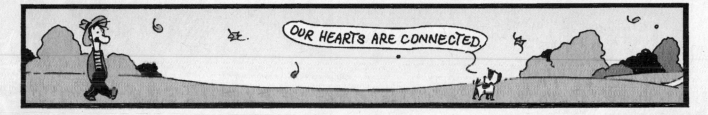

So part of their divine purpose is to help us.

But it always goes both ways. Because by living with humans,

dogs also grow in consciousness; it is reciprocal.

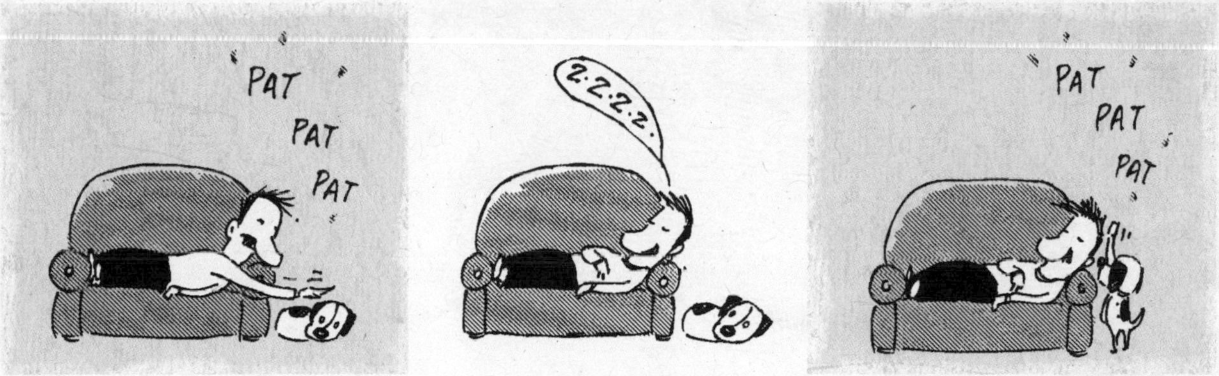
PAT
PAT
PAT
Z.Z.Z.Z.
PAT
PAT
PAT

Because dogs and cats still live in the original state of connectedness with Being, they can help us regain it. When we do so, however, that original state deepens and turns into awareness.

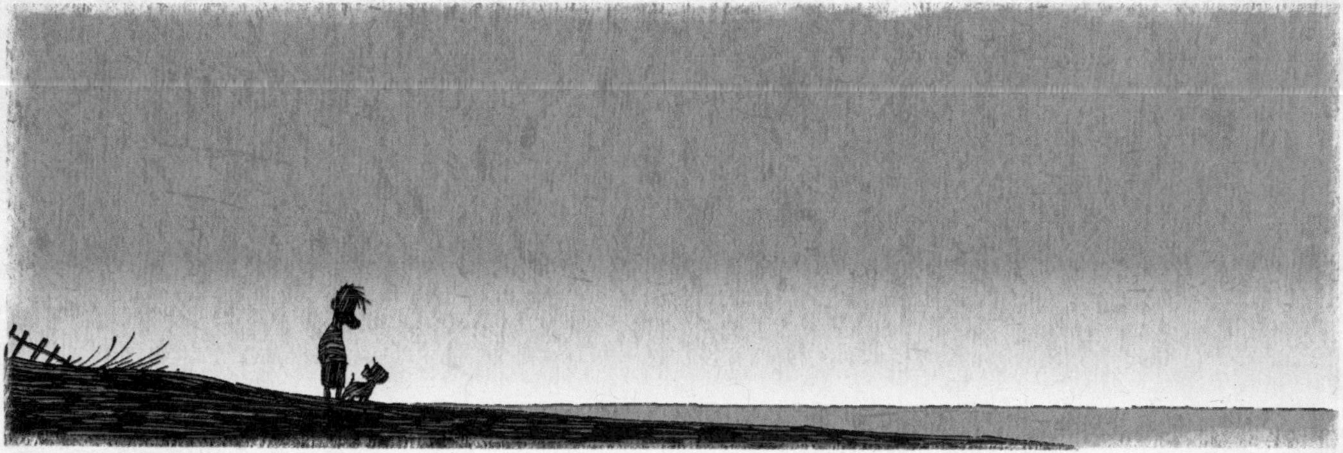

We don't fall below thinking,
we rise above it.

Nature will teach you to be still,

if you don't impose on it a stream of thoughts.

A very deep meeting takes place when

you perceive nature in that way, without naming things.

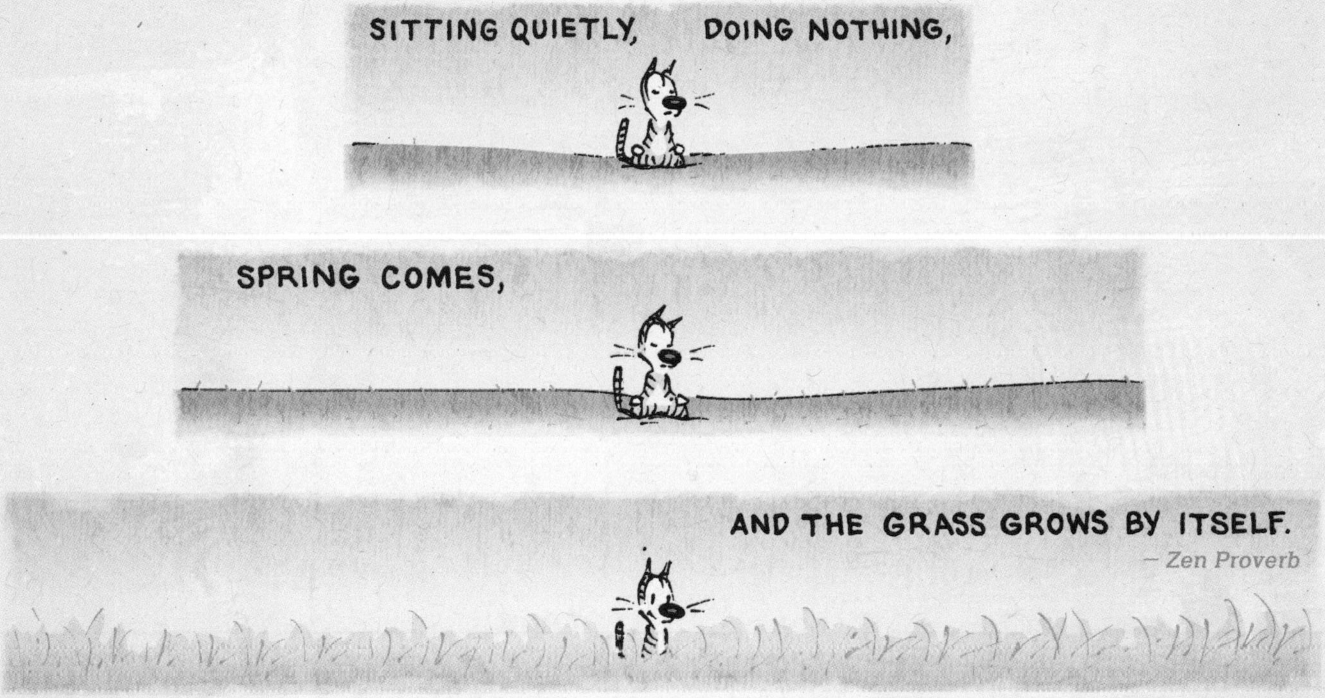

SITTING QUIETLY,
DOING NOTHING,
SPRING COMES,
AND THE GRASS GROWS BY ITSELF.
— Zen Proverb

When you don't cover up the world with words and labels,
a sense of the miraculous returns to your life that was lost
a long time ago when humanity, instead of using thought,
became possessed by thought.

A depth returns to your life.
Things regain their newness,
their freshness.

TWEET
TWEET
TWEET
CLAP
CLAP
CLAP
CLAP
CLAP
CLAP

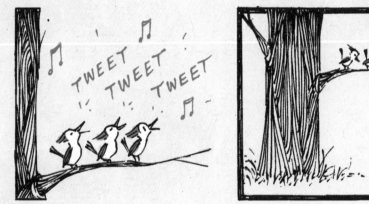

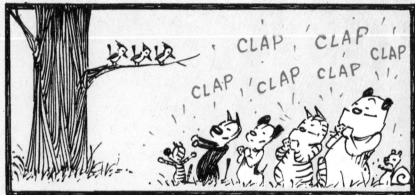

What is it that so many people
find enchanting in animals?
Their essence — their Being — is not
covered up by the mind, as it is in most humans.

And whenever you feel that essence in another,
you also feel it in yourself.

Every being is a spark of the Divine

or God. Look into the eyes of the dog

and sense that innermost core.

When you are present,

you can sense the spirit,

the one consciousness,

in every creature and

love it as yourself.

Love is a deep empathy

with the other's "Beingness."

You recognize yourself,

your essence, in the other.

And so you can no longer inflict

suffering on the other.

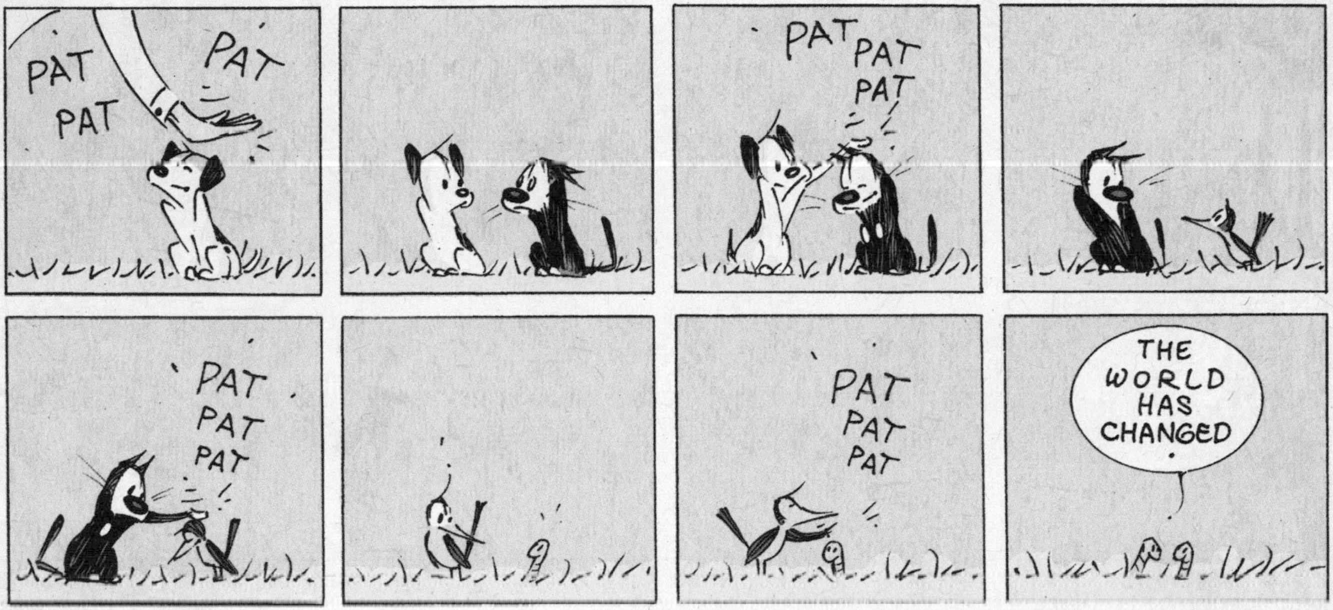
PAT
PAT
PAT
PAT
PAT
PAT
PAT
PAT
PAT
PAT
PAT
PAT
THE WORLD HAS CHANGED.

You are not separate from the whole.

You are one with the sun, the earth, the air.

You don't have a life.

You are life.

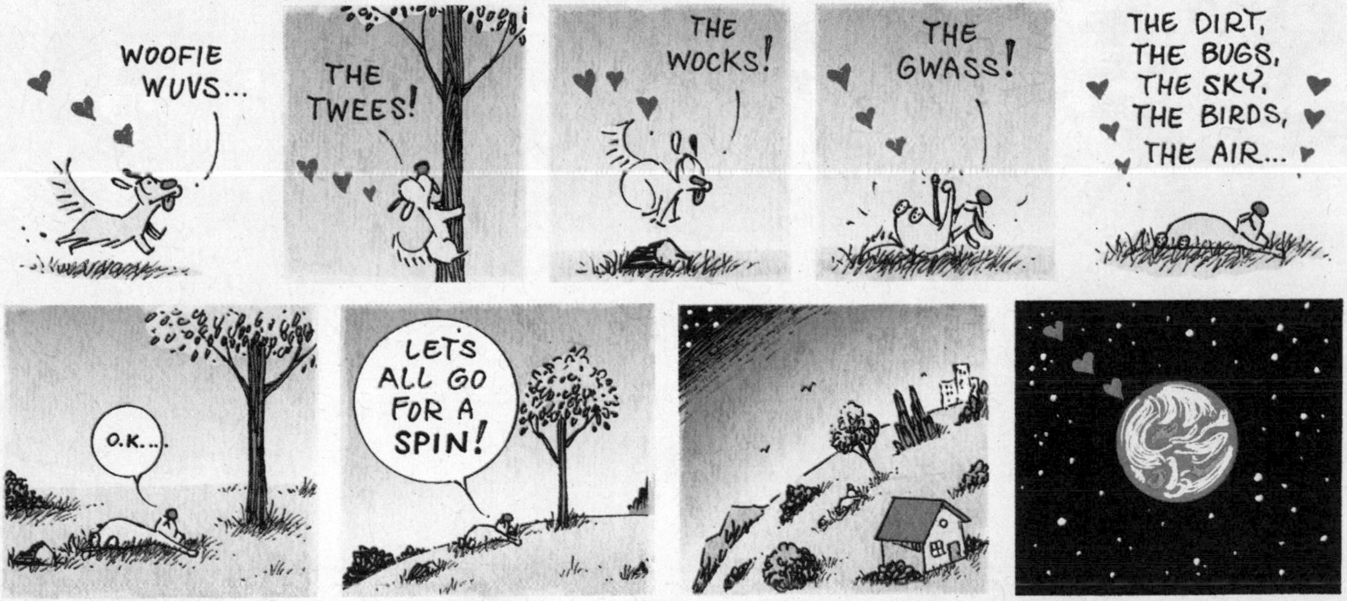
WOOFIE WUVS...
THE TWEES!
THE WOCKS!
THE GWASS!
THE DIRT, THE BUGS, THE SKY, THE BIRDS, THE AIR...
O.K....
LETS ALL GO FOR A SPIN!

The one life, the one consciousness,

takes on the form of a man or woman,

a blade of grass, a dog,

a planet, a sun, a galaxy....

This is the play of forms,

the dance of life.

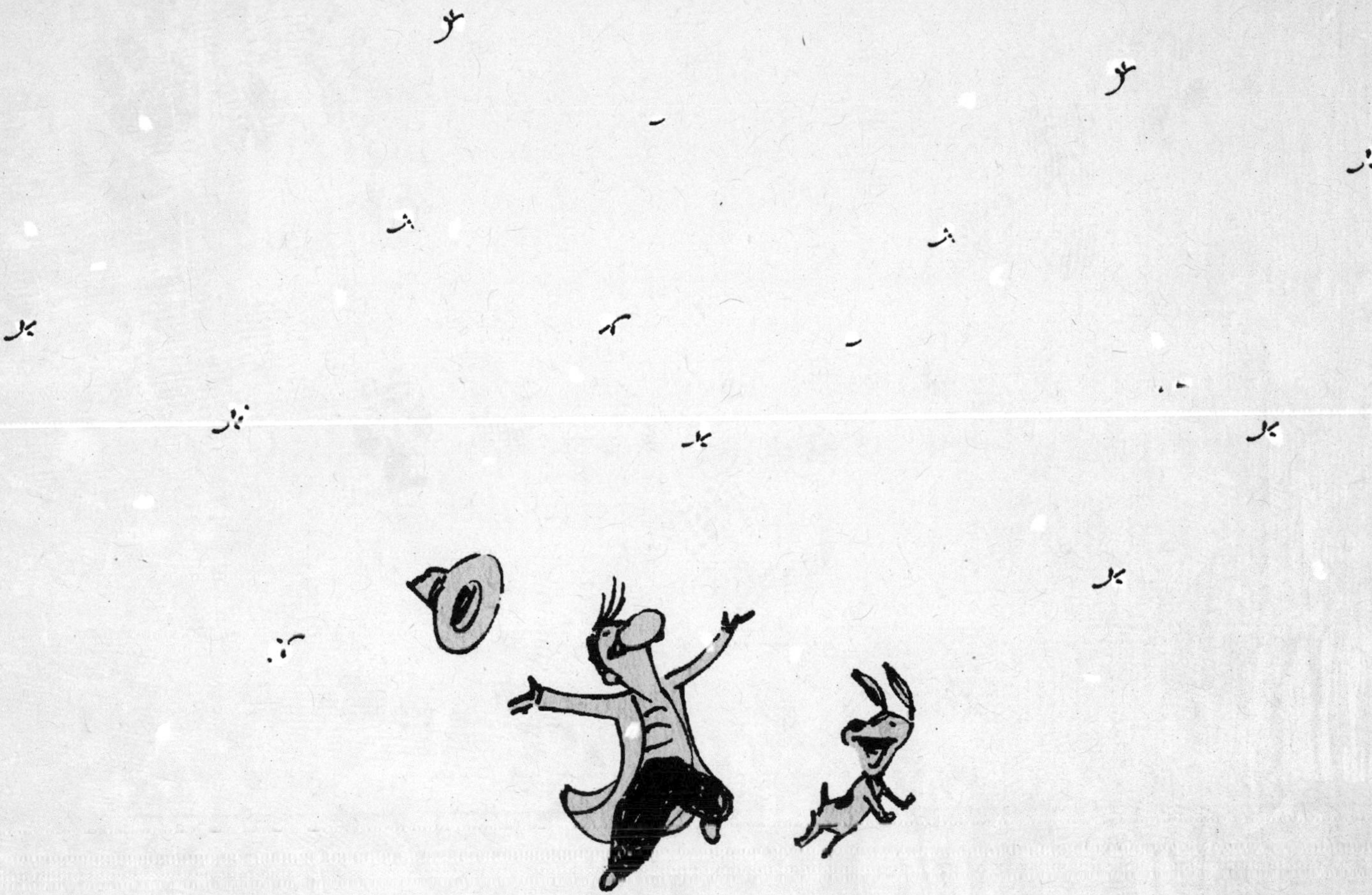

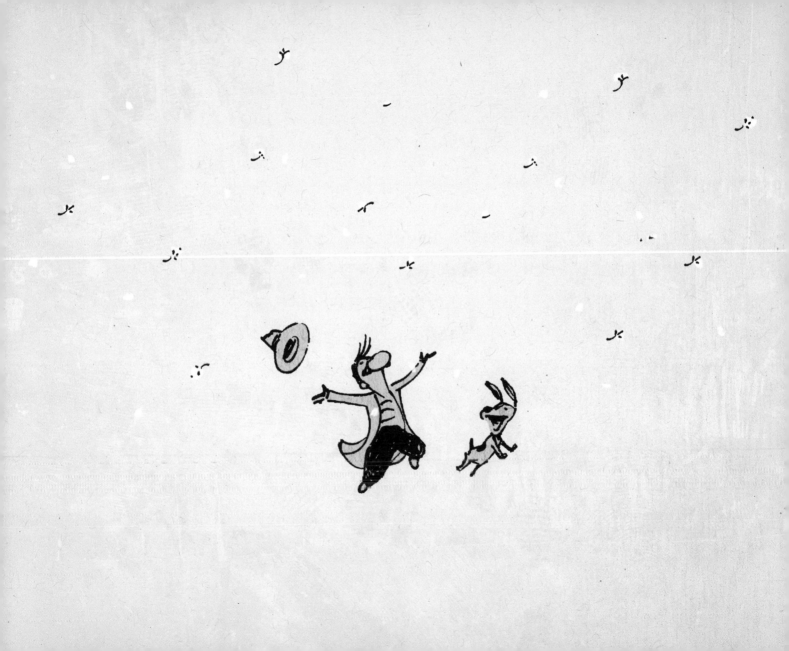

We are ultimately not separate, not from one another nor from any living thing — the flower, the tree, the cat, the dog. You can sense yourself in them, the essence of who you are. You could say God.

There is a term, a Christian term which is beautiful...

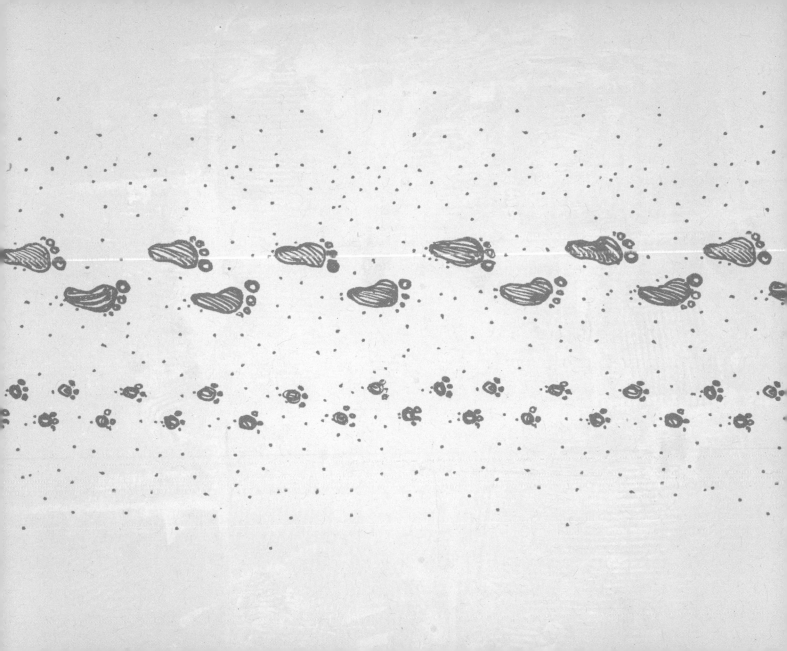

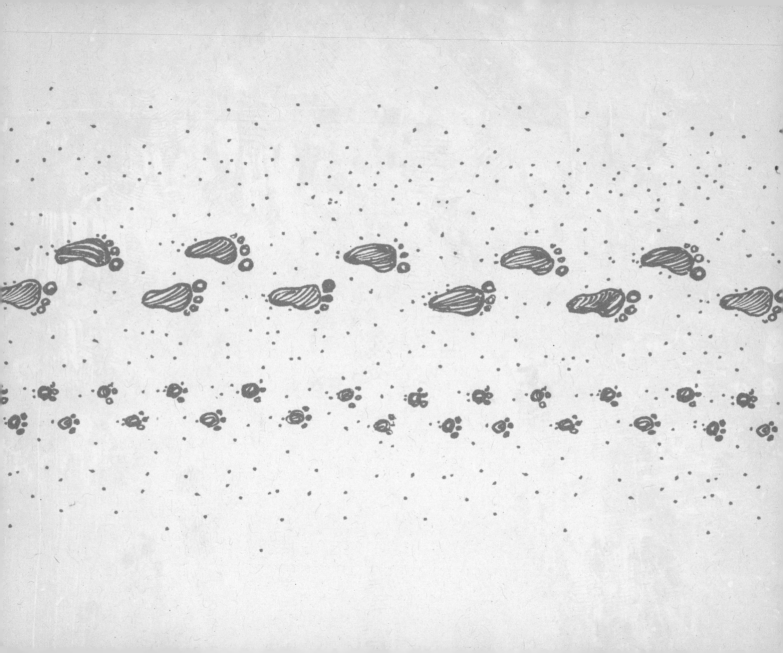

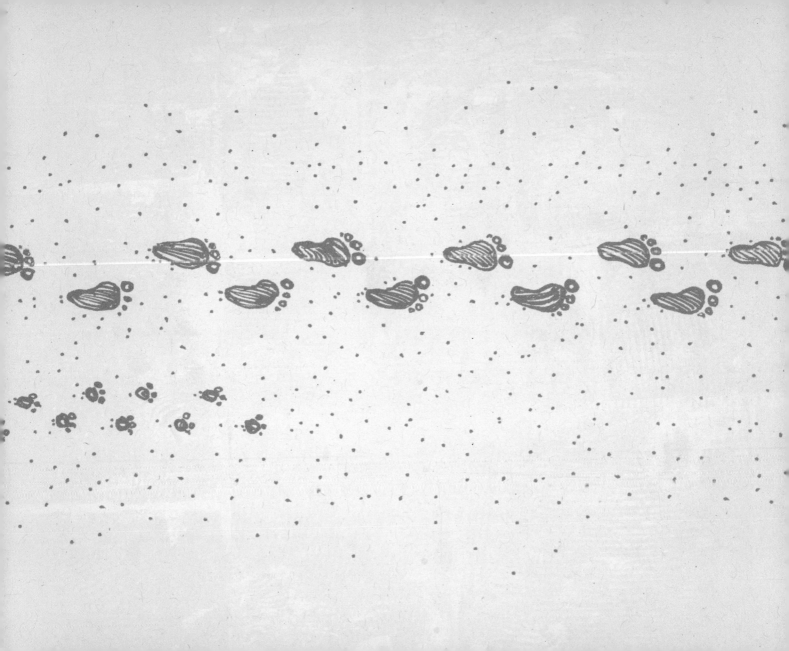

loving the Creator in the creature.

ECKHART TOLLE

Spiritual teacher and author Eckhart Tolle was born in Germany and educated at the Universities of London and Cambridge. When he was twenty-nine, a profound inner transformation radically changed the course of his life. He devoted the next few years to understanding, integrating, and deepening that transformation, which marked the beginning of an intense inward journey. Later, he began to work in London with individuals and small groups as a counselor and spiritual teacher. Since 1995 he has lived in Vancouver, Canada.

Eckhart is the author of the #1 *New York Times* bestseller *The Power of Now* (translated into thirty-three languages) and the highly acclaimed follow-up, *A New Earth*, which are widely regarded as two of the most influential spiritual books of our time. Eckhart's other works include *Stillness Speaks*, a book designed for meditative reading, and *Practicing the Power of Now*, which consists of selections from *The Power of Now*.

Eckhart's profound yet simple teachings have already helped countless people throughout the world find inner peace and greater fulfillment in their lives. At the core of the teachings lies the transformation of consciousness, a spiritual awakening that he sees as the next step in human evolution. An essential aspect of this awakening consists in transcending our ego-based state of consciousness. This is a prerequisite not only for personal happiness but also for ending the violent conflict endemic on our planet.

Eckhart is a sought-after public speaker who teaches and travels extensively throughout the world. Many of his talks, intensives, and retreats are published on CD and DVD. Most of the teachings are given in English, but occasionally Eckhart also gives talks in German and Spanish.

WWW.ECKHARTTOLLE.COM

PATRICK McDONNELL

Patrick McDonnell's *MUTTS* is a combination of his love of animals and his love of the art of the comic strip. Created in 1994, *MUTTS* now appears in over 700 newspapers around the world and on the web at muttscomics.com. *Peanuts* creator Charles M. Schulz called *MUTTS* "one of the best comic strips of all time." Patrick has received numerous awards for his art and animal advocacy. He has over 20 books in print including the *New York Times* bestsellers *The Gift of Nothing* and *Hug Time*.

Patrick is a member of the national boards of directors for both the Humane Society of the United States and the Fund for Animals. He lives in New Jersey with his wife, Karen; the formerly feral feline MeeMow; the still feral Not Ootie; and a new best friend, Amelie.

WWW.MUTTSCOMICS.COM

ALSO BY ECKHART TOLLE

A New Earth
The Power of Now
Practicing the Power of Now
Oneness with All Life
Stillness Speaks
Eckhart Tolle's Findhorn Retreat

ALSO BY PATRICK McDONNELL

Children's books including
The Gift of Nothing and *Wag!*

MUTTS comic strip collections including
MUTTS Shelter Stories: Love. Guaranteed.
and *The Best of MUTTS*

MUTTS: The Comic Art of Patrick McDonnell

NEW WORLD LIBRARY is dedicated to publishing books and other media that inspire and challenge us to improve the quality of our lives and the world. We are a socially and environmentally aware company, and we strive to embody the ideals presented in our publications. We recognize that we have an ethical responsibility to our customers, our staff members, and our planet.

We serve our customers by creating the finest publications possible on personal growth, creativity, spirituality, wellness, and other areas of emerging importance. We serve New World Library employees with generous benefits, significant profit sharing, and constant encouragement to pursue their most expansive dreams.

As a member of the Green Press Initiative, we print an increasing number of books with soy-based ink on 100 percent postconsumer-waste recycled paper. Also, we power our offices with solar energy and contribute to nonprofit organizations working to make the world a better place for us all.

Our products are available
in bookstores everywhere.
For our catalog, please contact:

New World Library
14 Pamaron Way
Novato, California 94949
Phone: 415-884-2100 or 800-972-6657

Catalog requests: Ext. 50
Orders: Ext. 52
Fax: 415-884-2199
Email: escort@newworldlibrary.com

To subscribe to our electronic newsletter, visit
www.newworldlibrary.com

ECKHART TOLLE TV

At this time of accelerating transformation, in response to what he calls
"the evolutionary impulse," Eckhart Tolle will be teaching in a pioneering new format:
monthly webcasts designed to catalyze spiritual awakening, foster community,
and provide clarity, guidance, and support. Now you have the opportunity to join
people across the globe to experience Eckhart's life-changing teachings.

As a member of Eckhart Tolle TV, you'll have the opportunity
to submit questions to Eckhart, participate in live recordings, view monthly
talks by Eckhart, receive weekly Present Moment Reminders,
join online group meditations, and more.

To start watching or to learn more, please visit
WWW.ECKHARTTOLLE.COM

eckhart
teachings

The work of Eckhart Teachings responds to the urgent need of our times:
the transformation of consciousness and the arising of a more enlightened humanity.
We organize Eckhart Tolle's talks, intensives, and retreats throughout the world. We also
record, license, publish, and distribute CDs and DVDs of his teaching events. In addition
to supporting Eckhart Tolle and the dissemination of his teaching, we are committed and
dedicated to serving the new consciousness and the awakening of all humans on the
planet. Behind the external form of what we do, and behind the business structure,
lies the company's and our true purpose: the union with the divine.

WWW.ECKHARTTOLLE.COM

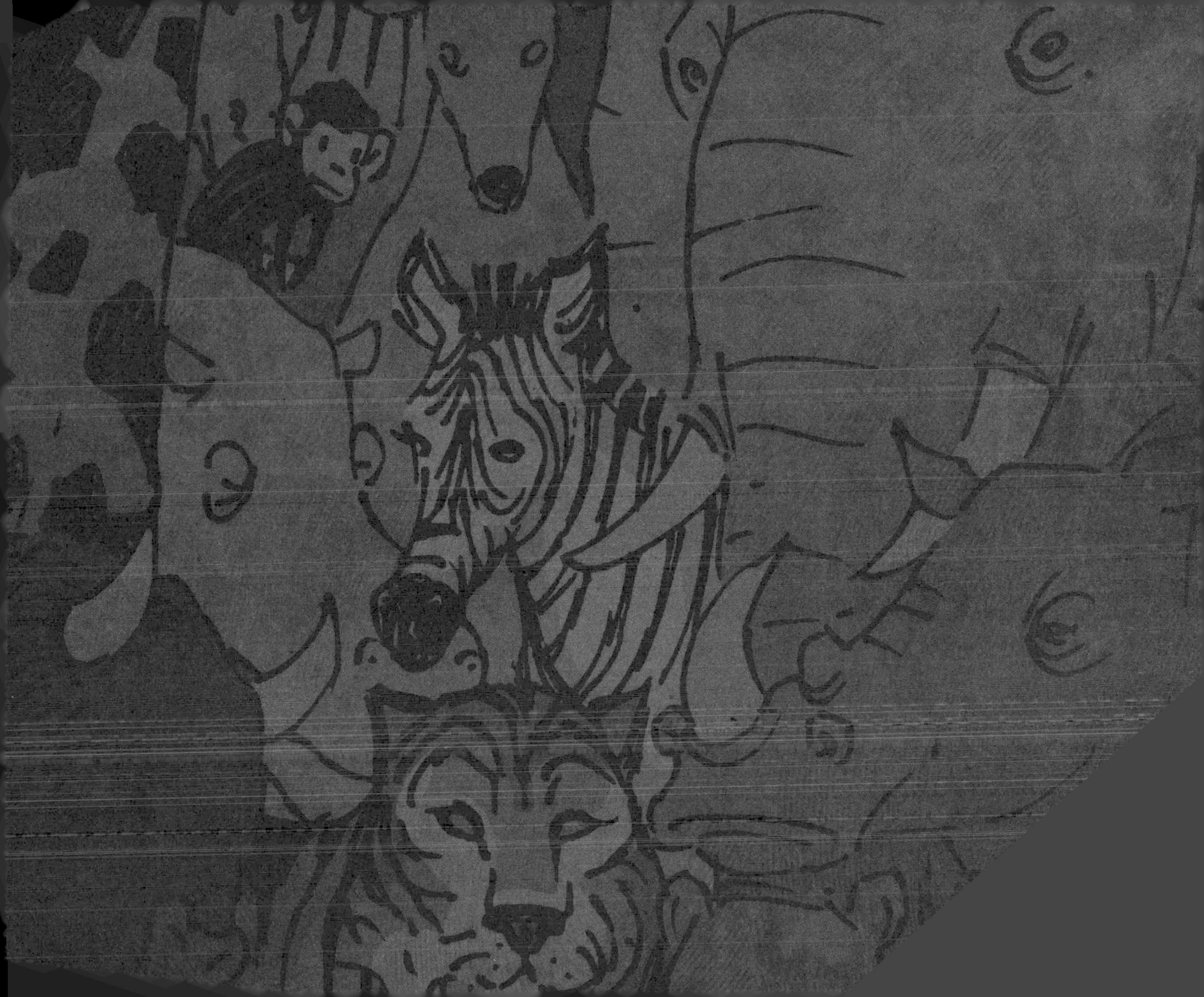

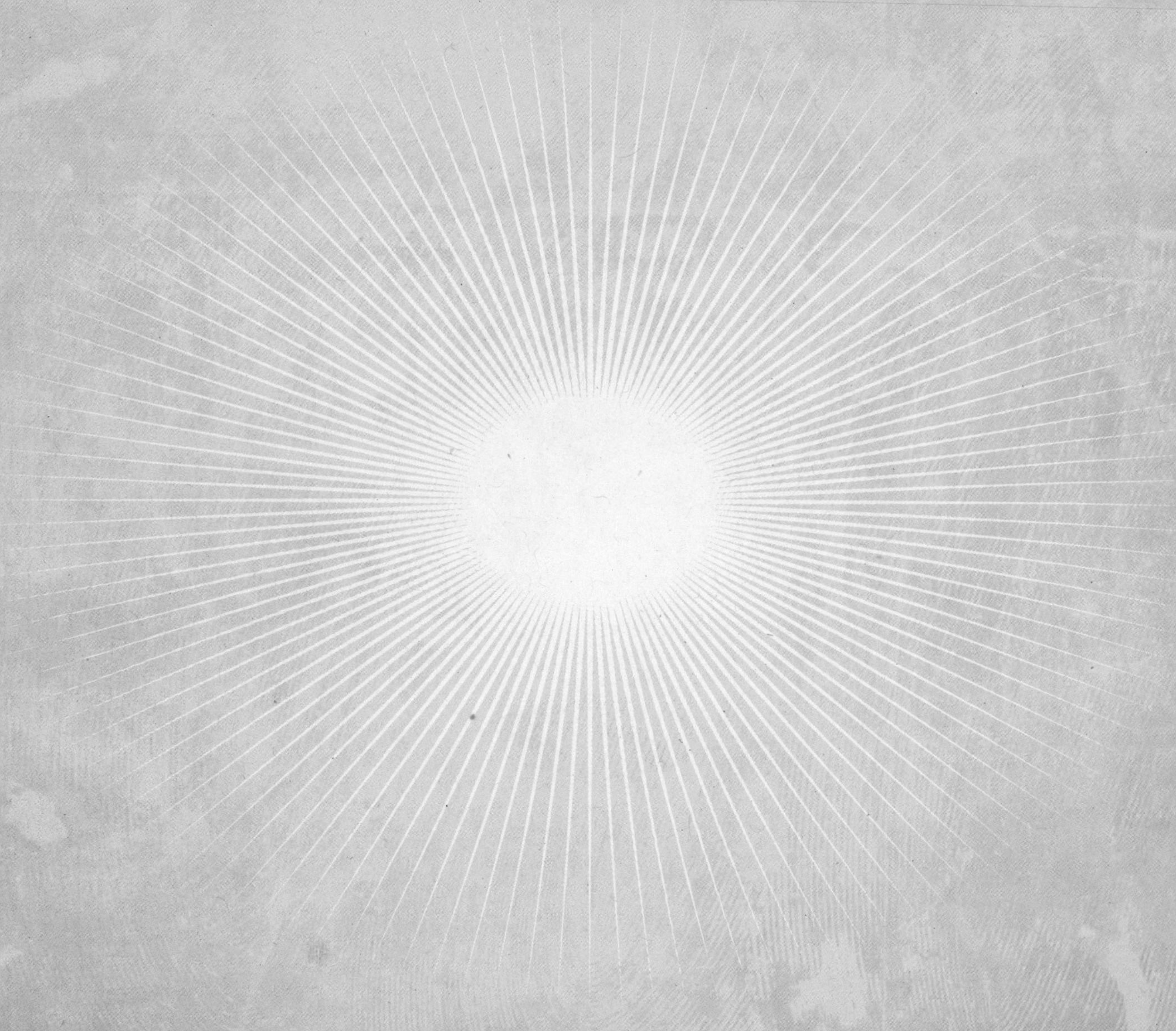